For o

Caro

Jeanne and Carl

Merry Christmas 2000

THE POET TREE

Jeanine Jensen

Cover artist - Eric Jensen

First Edition

First Printing • 300 • April 1996

Library of Congress Card Catalog Number: 96-94239

ISBN 1-57502-167-6

Printed in the USA by

Morris Publishing

3212 E. Hwy 30
Kearney, NE 68847
800-650-7888

A story in verse, long
kept locked in a box
beneath my desk.

Dedicated to:
My husband, Earl,
my sons Chris and Eric,
and my grandchildren
Derek and Whitney.

part I

Viking Song

In The Beginning

There was a rock, the loveliest,
I'd ever seen, a monument.

I touched the rock, beneath my hand
it seemed to warm, I felt a pulse.

I filled with love, it was returned,
and from it's heart, a fountain sprang.

I knelt to drink, the rock was God,
the water Love, and seas were filled.

A river formed, to share the love,
and carry it, around the earth.

A cloud took drops, to little birds,
and pretty flowers, came to life.

The fragrance fell, upon the wind,
All things were touched, and we were one.

My soul grew large, with all this love,
and splitting then, it became you.

I set you free, upon the waters,
knowing well, we will rejoin.

(for Earl)

part II

The Poet Tree Songs

Bedårende Sommerhus

Enchanted Cottage (to a Dane),
Appeared there in the Woods,
One day when I was walking by,
I glanced, and there it stood.

A house with soaring windows,
that seemed to reach the sky,
dappled with the sunlight,
through the green trees high.

I had the strangest feeling,
that it belonged to me.
A small sign said it was for sale,
and I knew that it would be.

I recognized this was the place,
as one in vision sees,
Where I could live, and write, and love,
With kin, the poet trees.

Where Little Girls Go

A grasshopper sings,
and through closed eyes,
for a fleeting moment,
I'm a child again.

Warm sun pours down,
wind stirs my hair,
and tall grass brushes,
my shoulders, as then.

Aimlessly, yet,
in thought I trail,
A dandelion held,
against my face.

I softly blow,
to tumble it,
and bend to touch,
some Queen Anne's lace.

A bird soars above,
my arms spread in mock,
and humming, I open,
a milkweed pod.

Then soundlessly,
I take my leave,
returning home slowly,
I wonder of God.

Family Tree

We didn't talk about it much,
and never with our friends.
When people tried, we'd brush them off.
The conversation ends.

Everyone did know, of course,
as so in a small town.
But families "good", as ours had been,
could turn the gossip down.

Grandma said that Daddy drank,
'cause something hurt inside.
I always wondered what, or who,
had made him want to hide.

He let us down in many ways,
broke promises, made sad,
yet never did we wonder,
if we were loved by Dad.

He tried to make it up to us,
by over doing things,
hoping then, that we'd forget,
embarrassments he brings.

Some give a label to our life,
"dysfunctional" they say,
We say, "It's just the way things were."
We don't whine anyway.

The Carnival

I remember the carnival,
coming each summer,
bringing more noise,
than heard in a year,
in a small town like ours.

The music was beautiful,
so were the signs,
posted just everywhere,
promising fun,
for a few, short, hours.

Somehow we went,
though there wasn't much money,
Mom thought it important,
to bring out the smiles,
on our serious faces.

Rita and I,
in fresh starched dresses,
braided hair flying,
skipped, stirring dust,
ahead many paces.

The Carnival (cont'd)

We snacked and took rides,
until we were dizzy,
laughing and screaming,
and waving at Dad,
from a ferris wheel high.

We tried not to notice,
when Dad slipped away.
Mom couldn't follow,
and just kept smiling,
as we flew by.

We walked home slowly,
just three of us now,
Carrying trinkets,
and treasures we'd won,
in small, sticky, hands.

Then tucked in our beds,
we talked of the fun,
and tried not to think,
how we felt when we saw,
Daddy leaving again.

(for Rita)

Eighteen

Eighteen –
Dad cried when I married so young.
He knew why I needed to go, but regretted.
He could hardly make it through the wedding
rehearsal, then fled.
It was very late when he came home.
The bars had closed.

After the wedding, when we drove away,
I watched him standing in the street,
holding me with just his eyes,
'till I was gone.
I never knew what he did then,
but I can guess.

Eighteen –
How we ever made it, I don't know.
We were two lost children in a big city,
for the first time, alone and scared.
Somehow we took care of each other.
God did the rest, teaching us to love.

It's been years now. Forty-three,
and I still marvel at how we grew.
Our love, so small at the beginning,
is now large, and growing yet.
We still hold hands in the middle of the night.

On the Wagon

One day, on a morn in spring
I woke to hear the phone's soft ring.
It was my Dad, who called to say,
Was I happy? Was I okay?

Of course, I said, and I am fine.
I asked him, how are you this time?
He seemed to search for words to say,
fearing I wouldn't listen anyway.

But he spoke on, and told me then,
he never planned to drink again.
He had not done so since my leave,
and could I try now to believe?

Could I forgive the many ways,
he'd let me down? What could I say?
Of course, but it takes time, I said.
Don't tell me, show me, wait instead.

Time passed, he sometimes slipped again,
but he did triumph in the end.
Without a drink, he lived for years.
I wonder, in heaven do they serve beers?

Little Sister

Our little sister, Rita's and mine.
Rita was seven, I was nine.
We didn't know then, how hard for her,
to be a baby, when we were "mature".

She must have felt lonely when we were teens,
perfumed, lipsticked, beauty queens.
We played with her like she was a doll,
showing her off when boys came to call.

Then one day we grew, and went away.
She had no sisters with whom to play,
at night in a room that held three beds,
Alone lay down just one little head.

Do you forgive us, sweet sister, dear?
Do you know we love you, even from here?
Do you know we're sorry we made you sad?
The only little sister that we ever had.

(for Twila)

The Subdivision Tree

I think that I shall never see,
this stick grow up to be a tree.

A tree whose leafy arms will spread,
to shade my swinging hammock bed.

A tree in which the birds may nest,
instead of on my porch light rest.

And that is really not the worst,
but I dare not set it to verse.

A tree under which we may lunch,
under shrubbery we can't munch.

They say that poems are made by fools,
and I refuse to break the rules.

(for our Herrington friends)

In Search of Praise

Darling, what do you say,
When you speak of me?
I often wonder this.

Some others boast,
it is plain to see,
of their talented Mrs. or Miss.

There's the wife,
Whose cakes,
are the best in the land.

There's the seamstress,
Who makes,
all her clothes by hand.

Among others,
the one,
Who makes anything grow.

And the gal,
With the figure
like Marilyn Monroe.

I feel,
very small,
beside brags such as these.

So if I do anything,
Well at all,
Would you just tell me, please?

My Hour In The Sun

Now in quiet contentment,
on my lounge I lie,
leery lest a rude cloud
Cross over the sky.

The unwritten sign, "Do not disturb",
has once again been hung,
and no one ever dare intrude,
my hour in the sun.

Projecting an invisible barrier,
I close my ears to sound,
eyes shut, warning all who pass,
tread lightly on the ground.

The telephone must not ring,
Children? I have none,
at least not while I'm claiming,
my hour in the sun.

What was that? A cookie?
Yes, take the whole darned bag,
but do not wake your brother.
Christopher! Don't nag!

The doorbell? Tell them I am sick.
A headache? I have one!
But that's the price I pay,
for my hour in the sun.

The Touch of Love

Touch my hand while you're asleep,
that I may know you're there.
With fingers still entwined let's wake,
another day to share.

Clasp my hands and hold them,
to your cheeks when in farewell.
Their touch sustains the parted hours,
'till they return in dwell.

Kiss these hands while joined in love,
the merest gentle brush.
Breathe softly warming them,
with tender words in hush.

Bonded through all time on earth,
fast will they remain,
enduring wholly light and dark,
happiness and pain.

For someday one will lie alone,
with outstretched hand in wait,
until again forever joined,
in constance with the mate.

My Way

Now I am what
my friends all think,
a non-conformity.

Though they don't say so
to my face,
it's pretty plain to see.

My tastes are inconsistent,
I will
admit to that.

In music I like classical,
yet blues and jazz
top that.

I do not like the moderate.
It must be hot
or cold.

I'm a beast when I am angry,
yet can be sweet,
I'm told.

I love to speak out frankly
of people,
and of places,

And note with satisfaction
their properly
shocked faces.

Last Star At Dawn

The one remaining star
still stubbornly,
And proudly displays her
brilliance for all to see.
Perhaps she doesn't know
that she's alone
and all this while she
vainly on has shone.
But, at last, it seems
she's opened wide her eyes,
for she flees to join
her sisters in the skies.

Little Boy Chris

Christopher has grown so big,
until I hold his hands,
and then I am reminded,
they are far yet from a man's

Square in shape and sturdy,
baked brown in the sun,
fingers short, with hang nails,
and a little mole on one.

Dirty hands that somehow,
never quite come clean,
and when he dries them on his towel,
another smudge is seen.

Hands that sometimes poke,
at one friend or another,
and yet grow gently kind,
when touching baby brother.

Innocent little hands,
when folded for his prayer,
bending mommy's head,
so they can stroke her hair.

Sometimes when I'm asking,
grown up things of him,
I just pick up his little hands,
remembering again.

Though he's more independent,
with every passing day,
he's really just a little boy,
and long will be that way.

While You're at Work

I wait for you in the sun,
and peace that I've not known,
all winter long,
settles upon me.

It's easier now that the wind is
gone,
And I find more patience,
than I thought,
I had.

You're more busy than I,
physically anyway,
my busy lies,
in word and thought.

We're different creatures,
you and I,
but still we get together,
now and then.

Discovering April

Turn your face into the wind,
breathe the gentle scent.
Let the stars into your eyes,
and thoughts be spent.

The moment is familiar,
and will be often so.
You'll not live long enough,
to see it go.

Again, as since you were a child,
you'll feel the poignant thrill,
on this, your best loved night,
discovering April.

Spring New

I wonder, will I ever reach
a day,
when spring will fail to take
my breath away?
I think not, rather I believe
we meet,
with wiser eye and heart
each time we greet.

Each vision, scent, and every
sound I hear,
grows sharper when I pass
another year,
and I embrace the blossoms,
sun and sky,
aware that they are part
of God, as I.

When Summer Comes

You can't go back?
Absurd, for every year I have returned,
to tread green velvet on the banks,
barefooted.

And always,
waiting there of course,
are yellow buttercups arranged just so,
a gift.

Seated then,
reappraising changeless things,
I accept the melodious welcome,
of the AuSable.

Wrapped in love I listen,
for the soft applause of birch leaves,
while pines bend forth to whisper,
"She is here."

Timeless, have no doubt,
nothing, even death would dare,
to block the path I walk,
when summer comes.

(for Jim, who loves the AuSable)

Summer's End

She left without goodby and fled,
to some unknown.
Knowing little, nor caring,
that we reached out to hold her,
she was gone.

Anxiously we waited,
unable to believe
she'd leave us so.
We kept a watch,
expecting recompense.

Then one day she returned,
no longer to withhold,
her warmth and love.
She stayed until it seemed
she'd faithfully remain.

Until, as if invisibly nudged,
reluctantly again,
she turned to leave,
replaced now
by a crisp successor.

Child By The Road

I don't know why I should have noticed her,
an awkward child with bony knees, all scarred.
A thoughtful little face, not beautiful,
too preoccupied to see my passing car.

Clutching a mass of yellow dandelions,
as shaggy an arrangement as her hair,
she intently kept attention to the field,
lest she miss another floral treasure there.

More than likely it was an indignant tear,
that accounted for the smudges on her face.
A taunting friend, a mother's reprimand,
is awfully hard at times to take with grace.

I couldn't hide a smile at her small nose,
a powdery gold that just matched her bouquet,
and at that moment, sensing my regard,
her face lit up, as lovely as the day.

(for Randi)

Prayers

One man prays,
for a raise to come through.
Another man prays,
just for work to do.

Still another asks,
to be shown the way,
to buy a new car,
from his meager pay.

A man without,
an auto begs,
just braces,
for his baby's legs.

A little girl,
prays for a horse,
while another cries,
"God, stop the divorce."

A mother's plea,
for her son at war,
"Please don't let him die."
"Bring him home once more."

Another mom prays,
for a son in jail.
"God, please forgive him."
"How did I fail?"

Whose needs are the greatest?
Who knows real despair?
I guess that depends,
on which one is your prayer.

The Analyst

Walk in the garden, fresh with morning
in hush,
and there, amid the green,
a single rose,
as red as cannot be described,
and velvet.
Inclined with just a touch of dew,
stirring softly,
glistening in the sun,
perfect.
Perfect? Can that be?
Foolish, true perfection exists not.
Where then, lies the flaw?
Test the sturdy stalk,
it breaks!
And, still in hand, inhale.
Ah yes, a rose,
each petal artfully wrapped around the first.
Where is the first?
What pattern has been used?
Spread them, search intently through each fold,
until the very heart exposed.
Why red?
Now look again.
Perfection? No!
Nor beautiful.
Cast it down in disappointment,
then search on,
flower to flower,
man to man.

A Grandma

A grandma is waffles and strawberry jam,
and greeting each day with a song.

A garden of pansies, and hollyhocks too,
where picking's allowed all day long.

She is one who will lie by your side through a storm,
telling stories until you're asleep.

One who never seems to notice,
tracks of muddy little feet.

A grandma is cinnamon rolls and warm bread,
and a quick smile to chase away fear.

A rocking chair, a lullaby,
and a voice that says "don't worry, dear."

She is one who sees the best in you,
when you really are quite bad.

For a little girl who for years would grow,
before knowing the love she had.

Our Fortune

Hand in hand,
we'll walk the fields,
yours strong and warm,
mine trusting and warm,
and ever flowing through them,
love.

Love,
the very strength,
with which we walk,
the only need we have,
that which men will seek and search,
down every road they turn.

The Willow Tree

In pursuance of some simplicity in life,
see the willow,
casually exquisite,
non-contending, non-demonstrating.

Knowing not that mother arms reach skyward,
offspring bend to touch the earth.

No purpose but to live,
no responsibility but to die,
and then without regret.

Not at the hand of self or other tree,
often not disease nor accident,
but quietly in unmeasured time it goes,
leaving nothing behind,
reuniting with the soil it's borrowed sustenance.

Quiet Time

Looks like a golden day, darling,
everything kind of waking and stretching
after the rain.

How many days has it rained?
I've lost count.

The fresh breeze will probably loose
the last stubborn leaves now,
and send them flippantly to wait the rakes.

Will you walk with me?
We won't talk, just have our own thoughts,
fingers touching.

Love

Love is a fair flower,
springing anywhere.
Holding out with gentle hands,
her precious gift to share.

Knowing not a season,
through sun or cloudy day,
she showers forth her beauty,
to all who pass her way.

Love is strong, and holds her head,
erect into a storm,
that we may lean on her when weak.
Her arms are always warm.

She forgives us what we are,
sees only what we mean,
and never seems to wonder,
if worthy we have been.

But though love seems unfaltering,
nourish her with care.
Give to her freely. Don't forget,
without her life is bare.

And should an unkind deed be done,
or thoughtless word expressed,
may we be understanding
and with forgiveness blessed.

Revenge

Stooping I beheld,
her lying there,
her body bent,
in obvious despair.

Ravaged at her peak,
of beauty great,
a lingering fragrance,
betrays her recent fate.

Her lovely white throat crushed,
deliberately,
uttered not a sound,
to comfort me.

Finally, through my sorrow,
came these words,
you've trampled my gladiola,
you dirty nerds!

Remember Beatniks?

The sea,
has confiscated me,
by its' beauty,
I'm taken in.

I know,
I'll never leave it now,
'cause man like,
I can't swim.

or

Other feet, have trod,
upon these sands,
these water washed pebbles,
laid on other hands.

Into their foot prints,
now my feet I put.
Oh Lord, I hope,
they didn't have athletes foot.

The Beat Goes On

Last night,
I called out to the winds,
they heard me not.
Tonight,
I called out to the winds,
they heard me not.
Tomorrow,
I will call out again,
with voice clear as a bell,
and then,
if still they hear me not,
I'll say,
winds, go to *hell*!

And On

The night was dark,
and no moon graced the skies,
no winking, twinkling stars,
disturbed my eyes.
No white cloud,
through the black velvet,
was showing.
I'd like it,
but I can't see where I'm going.
(Dig it, man.)

Labor Day Weekend

We grabbed brass rings,
and mounted leaves,
of shining red and gold,
riding bonus days of summer,
'fore the winter's cold.

We walked the beach,
now ours alone,
the tourists gone away,
gathering Petoskey stones,
along Grand Traverse Bay.

The bay wore diamonds,
after dark.
We danced along the pier,
the soft beams of a satin moon,
reflecting, like a mirror.

Next day we drove,
in silence,
loathe to say goodbye.
I held an acorn, keeping safe,
the season's last reply.

Tree Child

Run, little leaves,
skip and ride the wind.
In procession,
play a game of tag.
Accept your due,
you've shaded and adorned.
Fly free,
don't waste time or lag.

Once born,
an infant bud in spring,
you blossomed,
to a pretty child.
In youth you wore
a lovely coat of green,
in maturity,
your coat of colors wild.

Now gently loosed,
as in the plan of God,
you soar,
as promised you at birth.
'Till men unfeeling,
sentence you to fire,
denying your return,
to mother earth.

Autumn's Child

There is a tawny time I love,
When afternoon does hold,
the exuberant morning child,
who came,
in colors bright and bold.

There is a smokey time I love,
eves filled with glowing light,
distant sounds of laughter,
ring around,
bonfires bright.

Some say, a time of dying,
and yet, can that be true?
When my heart comes alive,
to greet,
October born anew.

Eric The Teen

Sometimes I feel I see,
into your heart,
its beautiful,
and filled with so much good.

You have a special smile,
when others grieve,
and give your time to those,
few people would.

Each morning when you rise,
so does the sun.
I sometimes think it is,
a part of you.

Why then some days,
do you pretend you're bad?
It leaves me feeling,
worried, scared, and blue.

On other days,
you're nothing but pure joy,
you treat me like your friend,
and not your mother.

I may have spoiled you some,
I must admit,
but you are an only child,
just like your brother.

Graduation

Seven hundred bodies young,
march in graceful cadence past,
to the poignant strains,
of pomp and circumstance.

Seated in a place above,
my eyes search rows of tasseled caps,
until they met the only face I saw,
my son, my sun.

(for both Chris and Eric)

College Chris

Yes, I love this kid with the long, stringy hair,
crowned with a band like Indians wear.

Such hair, to some, says he's bad and mean,
but I touch his hair, and it's soft and clean.

Frank, green, eyes and sun browned face,
seldom shaven, (a definite disgrace.)

A voice that speaks freely, to doubting ears,
all the truths he's uncovered in eighteen years.

Arrogant? Maybe, but earnest too,
defying all that's been proven true.

Still, I confess, my heart is won,
by his gentle eyes, as warm as sun.

A lean strong body, bare to the waist,
shirtless, in public (in very bad taste.)

Faded blue jeans, worn thin, then patched,
carefully stitched with fabric unmatched.

Why wear these things, with a closet full,
of college clothes, and sweaters of wool?

Bare feet, more dirty than some peoples shoes,
keep time to loud music of rock and of blues.

But my heart always warms when I hear those feet
come,
and I run to embrace my beautiful son.

Butterfly Unliberated

At times she beats her wings,
against the net,
with all the strength she has,
though delicate.

Then again she pauses,
knowing well,
her prison is a wall,
that cannot fell.

Silently she cries,
please understand,
I'd be content to sit,
upon your hand.

Your love would hold me,
better than your net,
if just your trust,
was large enough for that.

I only want to live,
with open wings,
I only want to choose,
what my life brings.

But his ears are not attuned,
to her soft voice,
and butterflies don't bite,
by their own choice.

So time will pass,
and she'll accept her life,
and maybe find some peace,
in ceasing strife.

Goodby Helene

The signs were there,
a year before you left,
still I didn't want to think,
that you would go.

If you did,
of course you'd turn around,
or you'd not be the person,
that I know.

Then one day the road,
that you had sought,
appeared as if you knew,
that it was there.

Testing ground to leave,
you did glance back,
I knew with that,
you surely wouldn't dare.

Suddenly a short cut,
came along,
and that was all you needed,
on that day.

You turned without a word,
upon the path,
crushing little flowers,
on the way.

The Scenic Route

"Rough road ahead,"
the sign there said,
I drive it every day.

But this time,
as I entered it,
I thought another way.

Too bad the roads,
of life aren't marked,
to warn us of the bumps.

Would we go,
another route,
or would we take our lumps?

I guess I know,
the answer,
at least I do for me.

The smoother,
straighter E-way,
is boring as can be.

Old Fears

A north wind is blowing,
I try not to hear,
but I do.

Walking window to window,
that old restless feeling,
comes back anew.

A skinny child once,
I had to stand twice,
to make shadows.

And grown-ups would say,
you'll sure fly away,
when the wind blows.

I'd watch at the window,
the happy, round, children,
hair tossed asunder.

But I wouldn't go out,
still won't, though I'm plumper,
(How plump? You'll just have to wonder.)

Sheltered

Can you keep the wind away,
                    my love?

Sometimes I think
if I could spend my days,
wrapped in your arms,
I'd live untouched,
                    by all bad things.

And with your lips,
pressed to my ear,
I wouldn't even
have to hear,
                    the sounds.

What more would one need?
I ask no more than this,
and yet, it is so much,
                    I'm told.

For there are those who say,
"And who are you,
to be so sheltered,
from the cold and pain,
                    we all must feel?"

And I say simply,
"Let me keep,
my lovely dream,
a fantasy,
                    lives a short life."

Sheltered

Can you hear the wind again,
my love?

Sometimes, with ivy
I'd once spent my days,
thought to preserve
it we neglected,

by all bad things

and only good like
passed by the fire.
Now, that even
I know anyhow

the sounds

Should we, should our need?
or could innocent than this
and yet of is so much

She told

So it, warm, from

Weather Alert

"What are you doing out
on such a day?"
Would surely be the question
asked of one.
Grey's the word, the sky
bleeds ice on all,
and everything in sight
will break
                                        and fall.

"Danger," warns the radio,
"stay in,"
and sipping coffee,
I look out to see
black branches, bare,
but for the frozen glass,
And watch an auto,
snails pace,
                                        going past.

For a moment I reflect,
my cozy state,
how fortunate that this,
need not touch me,
then sadly come aware,
I miss a thrill!
A walk perhaps? But then
I doubt
                                        I will.

Times Good and Bad

We've been down some rough roads together,
and shared many happy times too.

We've called when we needed each other,
knowing either will always come through.

We've worried through serious illness,
and sat by a hospital bed.

We all come to help with true willingness,
encouraging words are oft' said.

The phone still brings us together,
though we live far apart with the years.

The comforting voice of our dear friends,
rejoins us, and calms our worst fears.

(for Helen and Howard)

Christmas Card

Can Christmas be made,
to fit in a box,
or hung from the mantle,
in red woolen sox?

I have seen it contained,
in a snow flake white,
and dancing in flames,
of soft candle light.

I have heard it ring out,
in a church bell's gong,
and in voices singing,
a joyous song.

I have tasted it,
in cookie sweets,
in candy canes,
and home made treats.

I have felt it warm,
my heart each year,
in hugs and cards,
and words of cheer.

In a box? Of course,
with room to spare,
in the light, in the dark,
in the cool winter's air.

For Bette and Chuck

Save this summer, won't you,
'mong the many we have spent together,
old Cape Cod.

Someday, all too quickly come,
'twill be all that we have left,
a keepsake odd.

Funny, it can't go down as one,
upon which shone the golden sun,
yet warm again.

'Twas grey, as were the weathered docks,
and sturdy breezes stirred our hair,
hale as fishermen.

Fond friends, riding bicycles,
along the coast down winding streets,
past anchored boats.

Walking by proud dwellings square,
inscribed with tales of old sea captains,
and history's notes.

The children building sand castles,
with same grains scooped by unknown hands,
another day.

We leaving footprints on the shore,
where romance once had walked before,
and washed away.

For All the Giants

Sometimes you can talk to giants,
they're not mean.
They're more gentle than little birds,
and wiser too.

Giants don't like people to know,
that they are tender.
They growl a lot,
and try to scare you.

Sometimes I'd like to talk to people,
but I'm foreign,
giants understand, though
they're bilingual.

Giants are awfully hard to reach,
it takes patience,
but I spoke to one once,
and he listened.

Goodby

I met a patch of sunlight
in the forest.

It warmed me, lending comfort,
as it cleft.

As a man who loses riches,
is the poorest,

so the path ahead was darker,
when it left.

For All things fleeting

A balloon,
is just for a little while.

So beautiful and bright,
when it is new.

It soars, then plunges,
then soars again.

You can hold it for awhile,
but one day it will get away.

I've told the children,
not to cry when it's gone.

It would do well,
for adults to remember too.

Each Joy An Only Child

We had it All, for awhile
again,
suspended in a pool of
green,
and time stood still, no
where or when,
and warmed, and cooled us
in between.
Where was the place we
journeyed to?
May we go there another
day?
"No," says the wind. "You'll
start anew.
You'll have to go another
way.
You can't go back to
anywhere,
never will it be the
same.
Each moment is a treasure
rare,
an only child it will
remain."

(for Claire and Bob)

Florida Goodby

The airport sadness,
tells me that tomorrow,
I'll wake without,
the mockingbird, or you.

Thank heaven, when I packed,
I tucked away,
some special things I saved,
to see me through.

The morning sun will nod,
a cool good-day,
as if offended,
or I'd done him wrong.

But I've a beach,
within a grain of sand,
and soundless tapes will play,
the bird's sweet song.

Then, one by one,
I will unwrap these things,
and hold them,
for a little while again.

I'll squint my eyes,
and see a banyan tree,
or the ocean,
in a little drop of rain.

Sometimes while we sleep,
our souls will join,
to reminisce,
these happy times once more.

Then I may be awakened,
by a bell,
and rush to find you standing,
at my door.

(for Claire and Bob)

Class of '52

The school is new,
and grown, of course,
and things have changed,
since we passed through the doors.

Our number was small,
and is smaller yet,
having lost a few,
we'll never forget.

We've changed too,
we've grown a lot,
some lost their hair,
some gained a pot.

We've got some wrinkles,
round our eyes,
got some flab,
around our thighs.

And more, (a list
too long to tell),
since we last heard,
the tardy bell.

Still, when we get together now,
we say "you sure look good",
Our hearts see better than our eyes,
and that's the way they should.

(For My Classmates)

Wedding Song

I love you without doubt,
and without fear,
and will not hesitate to tell you
so.
No matter what life brings
while we are here,
my love is constant and will
ever grow.
I lay this love around you
like a coat,
to comfort you and keep you
from all harm.
Loosely, that you may in
freedom move,
while knowing it is there to
keep you warm.
My soul must live in this
imperfect house,
sometimes agitating,
causing pain;
But never will my love
bring hurt to you,
and faithful for all time,
it will remain.

(For Eric and Wilma on their Wedding Day)

Integration Trees

From where I sit, I see twelve trees,
Willows, by the creek.

I first thought them an ethnic group,
unto themselves they speak.

But then I saw a lovely elm,
In their midst he stood.

They didn't seem to mind,
that he was a different wood.

I stayed a while to listen,
to the conversation there.

Perhaps the elm was speaking,
of the willow's long green hair.

I couldn't understand, of course,
the language that they spoke.

They may have talked about the breeze,
or told a tree-toad joke.

Maybe they were singing,
gathered in a horde,
with frogs and locusts, birds and bees,
all in sweet accord.

Immodestly I then joined in,
and sang my person part,
never having a small doubt,
we all were one in heart.

Eric's Birthday Card

Twenty-five years ago today,
a new life was begun,
another angel soul on earth,
became my son, my sun.

I looked into his face so sweet,
and promised him that I,
would love, and teach, and care for him,
and comfort every cry.

I did these things with happiness,
a gentle man he grew,
and now he turns to give his child,
the same, from his heart too.

On Derek's First Birthday

Father, bless this little boy,
Who so fills our lives with joy.

Bless his Mom and Dad who share,
with grandparents his hugs and care.

Keep him safe from all that's bad,
Comfort him when he is sad.

Fill his little heart with love,
Light his way from up above.

As you've watched him through this year,
ever through his life stay near.

Use us any way you can,
to help him grow a gentle man.

Thank you, God, for using him,
to touch our lives with love again.

The Clown

There was another day,
another clown,
who lived in Wilma's heart
'till she was found.

I'm not sure Wilma knew,
she was within,
nudging to be freed,
to live again.

But clowns are patient,
as with children small,
and she could wait awhile,
before her call.

We first began to see,
her life take form,
when along with Wilma's child,
a clown was born.

The clown so long kept hidden,
came to life,
cut into birthday parties,
like a knife.

Wearing Wilma's body,
as her own,
she demanded costumes, makeup,
to be known.

Indeed there was no way,
she could be quelled,
with children everywhere,
under her spell.

She is their clown,
a piper, with a fife,
they parade with her, in joy,
and give her life.

(For Wilma)

Whitney

A year ago, a little rosebud,
pink, and fresh as dew,
appeared upon our family tree,
and opened, to be you.

The petal's blush became your cheeks,
the sky filled your blue eyes.
The sunshine lit your tiny face,
your nose was button size.

The Angels kissed your pretty lips,
and turned them to a smile.
The magic warmed our very hearts,
your beauty did beguile.

Your laughter filled our ears with song,
a special joy we knew.
Like spring again, we filled with love,
a new born love for you.

Just A Pause In Time

The calendar disagreed,
and yet no time had passed at all,
between us,
just put on hold,
like a telephone call,
then resumed.

No distance, or any happenings
in our lives,
made any difference.

We just picked up the conversation,
and the love,
where it had been.

No pretense, no attempt to impress,
no talk of accomplishments,
took place.

Just hugs and greetings,
and yesterday's joys continued,
with old friends.

(For Shirlee and Bob)

Limerick True

Remember the pancake fight gay?
The first one was tossed out in play,
then we, all four,
had an all out war.
(The birds had a feast that day.)

Or the chocolate mousse story,
which took place in a posh eaterie,
When a waiter haute,
a domed silver try brought,
raised the cover,
for we four to see.

Our wondering eyes beheld,
the creation on silver tray shelved,
'twas an artful, brown, coil,
on raspberry royalle.
(What happened then, I hate to tell.)

We completely lost all control,
at the sight before our eyes,
the laughter just came,
and much to our shame,
while the waiter haute gasped in surprise.

Now I could go on to the night,
when Roy tripped and seemed to take flight,
he slid 'cross the table,
and still he was able,
to keep his filled glass upright.

I suppose you'd have to have been there,
we were, I am happy to say,
there were many more times,
and many more rhymes,
that space will permit anyway.

(For Glada and Roy)

Limerick Time

Apparently the pancake hadn't gone
English and was tossed off in play
without all fear
and on all our new
That sparkled a past that didn't

The flapjack moused aloft
which took place in a post anthem
within a motor hauler,
a bored singer, he thought,
without the rower
as Jane to see

The

Lisa's Birthday Card

Candles light the night,
and sunshine warms the day,
and children touch our lives,
in a special sort of way.

They warm us with a smile,
and point our way with love.
God's little ambassadors,
from the land above.

Julie

So little, only knee high,
so young yet, only one,
yet you command attention,
as the shining, morning sun.

So innocent, a baby,
so gentle, loving too,
yet as spirited a maverick,
as I will ever view.

So curious, your seeking,
so bold, each move you make,
yet I believe your life will be,
a happy birthday cake.

Old Friends

Often we,
have heard folks say,
a friend,
is like an old shoe.

It just,
occurred,
to me today,
that what they say is true.

The friends,
we've had,
a long, long, time,
are never just a fad.

New style,
friends,
will never feel,
like old ones we have had.

Friends,
like shoes,
should fit you well,
(a most important role.)

Shop carefully,
before you choose,
be sure you check,
their soul.

(For Francois)

For Paul

Paul didn't really leave us,
on that sad day in April,
he just left behind a body,
that no longer served him well.

When we all get together,
I know that he's there too,
enjoying every minute,
the way he used to do.

I feel we still can talk to him,
and know that we are heard,
and though he answers silently,
we hear his every word.

His family and his friends just wait,
(and none too patiently,)
until our souls, reborn again,
will share eternity.

(Mar. 30-29) (Apr. 15-87)

Jesus Loves you, Don and Shirley

(I do too, if you want to know.)

I'll meet your plane,
holding high my sign,
for all to see,
as they come and go.

Yes, Jesus loves us.
(Maybe more when we are fun.)
Can't we just be real,
and sincerely feel,
amused,
at religious puns?

Honk if you love Jesus,
(I see along the road.)
Do the geese comply,
as they're passing by,
on their way,
to winter's abode?

Repent Ernie and Judy

The end is near!
Another sign to make you quake in fear.

Another airport meeting afternoon,
I hold it high to warn you of your doom.

The passengers go by in single file,
A priest observes my message with a smile.

Then you de-plane, and look around for me,
The one who has proclaimed your destiny.

And I don't doubt you really do repent,
as you rush to hug your friend who's time was spent,

awaiting
your
late
flight.

The Promise

Spring came again,
and we walked down,
beside the lake,
now flowing free.

It woke and stretched,
in sandy bed,
greeting morning,
happily.

Chuck said, come spring,
he would return,
at nesting time,
before the noon.

Without a word,
we scanned the blue,
till our eyes met,
a single Loon.

The water hushed,
that we might hear,
his morning call,
above the wind.

Through whispering pines,
I barely heard,
Earl's soft reply,
"I've missed you, friend."

For Chuck
(5-18-30) (10-22-89)

August Night

Remember when we were last together,
playing games in the night,
because we couldn't bear to end
the day?

There wasn't a ray of light anywhere,
except the stars.
You said you had never seen
such darkness.

The same stellar display we saw,
as children,
was telescope clear, larger, closer,
that ever.

Maybe it's because our time has grown,
more precious now.
Maybe it's because our older eyes
see better.

(For Za and John)

Mom

I pray so, now that Mom is gone,
her dearest dreams came true,
that God gave her a just reward,
for all she tried to do.

She worked so hard at nursing,
and caring for the ill.
Then came home tired, to care for us,
and all our needs to fill.

She never asked much for herself,
just did her best each day.
At night, the things she read in books,
were her sweet get-a-way.

She never saw the ocean,
except in her mind's eye.
She dreamed of seeing mountains,
reaching to the sky.

I look around at all I have,
and in my heart I pray,
that Mom has this, and even more,
with every passing day.

Ponzo

I never meant to like you,
I never did like cats,
they always pounced,
and scratched at me,
(I'd just as soon pet rats.)

But then you started coming by,
just sitting for awhile,
and watching me,
through large, green eyes,
(did I detect a smile?)

One day you started speaking,
I had to answer you,
we talked together,
quite awhile,
(as cats are prone to do.)

You told me that you liked me,
a trick that never fails,
and inching closer,
whispered, purred,
(can cats caress with tails?)

Then finally in a brave move,
you nuzzled to my hand,
this touching gesture,
warmed my heart,
(could I <u>not</u> be your friend?)

Part III

God's Song

God's Song

The willow wept for the children,
who died without hearing the song.
Tears washed down lovely green lashes,
and splashed upon the ground.

It was there in the drum of the thunder,
on the wind, all around in the air,
but they weren't attuned to the soft sweet sound,
nor even did they care.

Then an old man, who heard it quite clearly,
stopped to comfort the tree with his love.
Then, trustingly heeding the message,
ascended a light from above.

Now the sun shines from out of his blue eyes,
and gives to the children new life.
And the song comes again from the heavens,
reborn in the voice of a fife.

(for God)

Jeanine Jensen has written poetry "always". She was born Jeanine Sorenson in Grayling, Michigan, where she lived until she married Earl Jensen, then moved to the Detroit area. They have two sons, Chris and Eric. Most of Jeanine's years were spent in Troy, Michigan, where she was active in Community service. She served many years on the Troy Historical Commission and as a museum volunteer. Earl and Jeanine now live in their beloved "Enchanted Cottage" [Bedårende Sommerhus, Danish.] at Guthrie Lake near Gaylord, where she writes surrounded by nature and "poet trees". She has published single poems and songs, and her work was included in two anthologies of the National Library of Poetry. This is her first complete book.

Index

Part I

Part II

Part III

To order additional copies of The PoetTree complete form below:

Name ______________________________

Address ______________________________

City, State, Zip ______________________________

Day Phone ______________________________

______ copies of The PoetTree @ $7.95 ea. $ ______

postage and handling $1.50 ea. $ ______

6% tax $ ______

amount enclosed $ ______

make checks to: Jeanine Jensen
send to: 11396 Enchanted Dr.
Frederic, MI 49733

- -

To order additional copies of The PoetTree complete form below:

Name ______________________________

Address ______________________________

City, State, Zip ______________________________

Day Phone ______________________________

______ copies of The PoetTree @ $7.95 ea. $ ______

postage and handling $1.50 ea. $ ______

6% tax $ ______

amount enclosed $ ______

make checks to: Jeanine Jensen
send to: 11396 Enchanted Dr.
Frederic, MI 49733